DIFFICULT PEOPLE

Dealing With Difficult People At Work

Disclaimer

This eBook is for educational purposes only, and is not intended to be a substitute for professional

counselling, therapy or medical treatment. Nothing in this eBook is intended to diagnose or treat any pathology or diseased condition of the mind or body. The author will not be held responsible for any results of reading or applying the information.

Table of Contents

About Colin G Smith

For over ten years now I have been driven to find the very best methods for creating effective personal change. If you are anything like me, you're probably interested in simple and straight-forward explanations. Practical stuff that gets results! I am a NLP Master Practitioner, writer & author who has written several books including:

- Boost Your Mind Power: 99+ Awesome Mind Power Techniques

- EFT Tapping: How To Relieve Stress And Re-Energise Rapidly Using The Emotional Freedom Technique

- Neuro-Linguistic Programming NLP Techniques - Quick Start Guide

How To Deal With Difficult People At Work

It's a well known fact that dealing with difficult people has its own complexities. Nothing is clear cut when we are dealing with emotions, and when emotions are on the rise, logic flies out the window. When dealing with difficult personalities, sometimes we get the urge to lash back and give them what they deserve. In the business setting, the lack of better management of difficult people can result to inefficiencies, delays and decreased productivity.

- Be calm. Showing your frustration and venting it out is not the best way to deal with difficult people at work. Polite conversation has its own advantages. Pulling a tight rein over your emotions shows that you are rational, respectable and in control. You are more likely to think clearly and focus better on what can be acted upon. Avoid head butting and aggravating the problem especially when you find that the instigator is your superior.

- Prepare for interaction and actively listen. Organise the data that you would need. Support your presentation with facts. Resist the urge to fight back with difficult people when you can win an argument. Listening and asking questions will make the interaction more productive and lead to better solutions.

- Be compassionate. Never embarrass anyone. Be silent when necessary. The willingness to understand and a sincere attempt in diffusing what is otherwise a volatile situation makes one the better person without having to be defensive. Try to understand the anxieties he or she is going through. Difficult people at work need more than the usual understanding.

- Apply a self-assessment. Begin by inspecting and asking yourself if the difficult people are making things purposely hard for you or are you being overly sensitive to the situation? Is there a pattern? Do you get along with the others? Perhaps it's not the difficult person, it could be you.

- Consider cultural or regional differences so don't be too hasty in jumping to conclusions. Sometimes it can be more than just a personality collision. This is the most crucial part of how to deal with difficult people where you need to be properly oriented with the rules and policies of the company to provide you the support as each will have its own unique set of guidelines.

- Get into the root cause by asking questions. This simple (just asking open-ended questions) yet effective strategy would likely get you the solution you are looking for when dealing with difficult people. Ask for specifics instead of being satisfied with generalities and vague statements.

- When you are calm and show respect to others, refusing to be pulled into the games of difficult people, you will become more successful, your coping mechanisms will become stronger and you're more likely to achieve a win/win outcome.

Improving Communication Skills at Work

One of the most valuable skill-sets you can bring with you to a job is good communication skills. Meaning you are able to communicate efficiently through email, on the phone, or in person. When you practice good communication skills at work, it is easier to accomplish goals in a team. Even the best communicators could use some improvement and there are several ways you can improve your communication skills at work if you take the time and effort to do so.

Learn How to Listen

While half of communication involves expressing yourself, the other half involves listening to what others have to say. Too often, someone will be so absorbed in their own needs that they will not listen when someone is trying to tell them something and will instead try to push their own agenda on others without considering the thoughts and feelings of the people with whom they are trying to communicate.

When you are listening to someone, pay attention to both the words they are saying and nonverbal cues that show how they are feeling. Do not interrupt the other person; let them express themselves fully while giving cues that you are listening attentively. When the person is done talking, repeat back the main points to make sure you understand what the other person was saying; this way they will know you were listening carefully.

Be Aware of Your Nonverbal Communication

You may know what you want to say with your words, but you may not realise how others are interpreting it. You need to make sure that your nonverbal communication matches up with the message you intend to convey. This means that you should be aware of your eye contact, posture, facial expressions, and gestures or the way you are positioning your arms. As you may find if you observe the nonverbal communication skills of effective communicators, the best nonverbal communication involves direct eye contact, a relaxed yet upright posture, an enthusiastic and approachable facial expression, uncrossed arms, and non-threatening gestures that match up with the feeling of whatever it is that you are saying at the time.

Be Flexible With Modes of Communication

Everyone prefers to communicate with a different mode of communication, whether it is over email, over the phone, or in person. If you demonstrate that you can communicate effectively in all of these ways, people will feel more comfortable communicating with you because they will see that you want to be accommodating to their needs. No matter how you are communicating, you should always make it a point to express yourself professionally so that people will respect you and trust your competency as a communicator.

The Seven Types of Difficult Personalities

Workplace, community or even home – difficult people exist everywhere. It could be your co-worker or boss, your next door neighbour or the person next to you in bed, the person behind the glass window as you cash in your cheque, or the voice on the other line when you call for a doctor's appointment. It is not gender-specific, and social status does not predetermine it, but it does a good job in poking at your frustration, raising stress levels and overall, just elicits feelings of negativity.

Some would call them bullies, whiners, argument-seekers, know-it-all, slackers, people-pleasers, or even pessimists; in a nutshell, dealing with difficult people is an everyday occurrence.

The Hardcore Bully

"I will not budge; you will move for me." "I will lash out when I feel threatened by others." "You won't know what's coming to you." Difficult personalities like the bullies are hostile whether overtly or covertly (yes, there are subtle ways of hostility), abusive or just downright intimidating. At the receiving end, one feels discriminated against, regularly criticised on very trivial matters; continuous attempts to undermine you and your position, status and worth. In a group setting, you will be singled out and given different treatment. For example, the others can very well get away with almost anything, but if you make the slightest error, however small, it will be held against you.

Mr. Know-It-All

"I am better than you." "I know what's best for you." "I will tell you what you need to know." "I know more than you do." The Experts, as we could also call them, come in two kinds; the capable one who is competitive, productive, self-assured, and confident, and the person who just pretends to be an expert, but only knows a little of this and a little of that.

Willie The Whiner

"I don't like it." "I am not changing my work; it looks completely fine to me." "I am not the problem, they are." "Why are things so slow around here, other companies are doing it at lightning speed." Dealing with difficult people showing this tell-tale sign can push you past frustration. It saps your energy and just makes things terribly exhausting. They tend to be the chronic complainers at work. These difficult people often see the point, but their complaining is ineffective because the blame is always pointed to someone else. The complainers never seem able to rectify the situation and are just too happy to call out what was done wrongly.

The Pessimist

"I don't like dealing with it." 'This is not going to work." "This is too difficult." "Why change strategy?" These are the naysayers. They like their comfort zones and are constantly anxious that something will go wrong. This could result in the shooting down of ideas of others and clinging on to the status quo. A characteristic of this type of personality is the *unenthusiastic mindset.* One would often hear them say, *"Yes, but..."* In effect, having them as friends or co-workers could stir one's residual doubts.

The Gossip: The Credit Grabber: The Delegator

Difficult people at work can be a mix of the following; The

Gossip; The Credit Grabber and The Delegator. In almost every workplace, you will come across all three.

The Gossip seems to have something to say about everyone and wants to share with everyone! Dealing with this type of person can work both ways. Yes, it is good to hear news through a more informal channel, but one has to exercise an effective filtering process as the information contains the truth and embellishments.

The Credit Grabber wants the spotlight and recognition all to himself. He would accept all the praises without acknowledging other people's input and claim all the glory. How often would you suggest an idea to your boss, and he would turn it around and present it as his own? Credit grabbing is commonplace in many organisations.

The Delegator would spend his time assigning tasks. This has nothing to do with the valid reason to delegate work to others; it is about those who either can't do it or do not want to do it. Often a manager, these difficult people will spend a little time actually doing work, but manages to look busy.

How To Communicate
With Difficult People

Interacting with difficult people at work is often challenging and can add more to the stress on top of work tasks. Unfortunately, they are in our faces constantly, and we can only do so much to avoid them. So, how do we deal with these people, especially how do we communicate with them?

As hard as it is, do not take things personally. Step back and gain perspective on things. This will help give you an insight into the person's intentions. Ask questions rather than make assumptions. Use phrases like, *"I want to ensure that I understand things correctly, you are saying..."*

Keep it objective and logical. Avoid injecting opinions unless asked; be more factual. Your opinion will tend to spark an argument with difficult people. Do not insist on having them see your point of view.

Do not be intimidated, but do not be on the offensive either. Be rational in your approach and point towards the deed rather than the doer. So, if your supervisor calls you a dismal failure, acknowledge the error without being defensive saying, *"It is true a mistake has been made and I thank you for your constructive feedback. This will be helpful in reducing further errors."*

It is also best to seek permission when you want to provide feedback, especially when the feedback is for a subordinate or someone in the same authority as you are. This gives people a chance to handle confrontations in an even manner. Be straightforward, and you can use something like, *"I am discussing this with you because it is something that needs to be addressed for the success of this project."*

One can also use nonverbal communication when dealing with difficult people at work. It's been observed that 93 percent of our communication is expressed through nonverbal cues. Your interactions with people should take conscious consideration of the body language, facial expression, spatial comfort and eye contact. The nonverbal may say more than the verbal. If a person's action is the opposite of what he or she is saying, then chances are that you should be inclined to pay more attention to the nonverbal.

Regardless of how it is delivered, verbal or nonverbal, communicating with difficult people requires practice and patience. The more you exercise your observation skills, the more you become effective in handling difficult interactions. Practice until you have reached new levels of confidence in dealing with difficult people at work or difficult personalities in general.

How to Manage Difficult Conversations

If you have ever found yourself in the middle of a difficult conversation, or you have been faced with the burden of needing to start a difficult conversation with somebody, you know how uncomfortable it feels. You may face a risk of losing something that is important to you, whether it is a job, money, or a relationship. It helps to know how to manage a difficult conversation before you begin so you can complete the conversation as productively as possible while causing the least amount of damage and staying true to your goals.

Identify the Goals of the Conversation

Before you begin a difficult conversation, you should clearly identify goals you wish to achieve during the conversation, rather than acting with anger and not planning out your approach beforehand. If you have some time to think about what you want to say, you will express yourself more articulately and logically, which will help the other person take you seriously.

Don't *"Push"*

Often when someone is having a difficult conversation, they will try to push their feelings and opinions on others, which just makes the other person feel attacked and causes them to get defensive without really listening to what the first person is saying. Instead of placing blame, you should frame the discussion in the context of how you personally feel because of specific words and actions the other person directs towards you. This way, you are simply opening up and sharing a problem rather than attacking someone else when they aren't prepared for it. When you share your feelings in a nonaggressive manner, the other person will genuinely want to understand where you are coming from and will want to help solve the problem.

Remember to Listen

When you are having a difficult conversation, you should make sure to let the other person express their point of view so they will understand that you want to work the problem out with them and not just complain without being willing to try to work things out. Once you are ready to give the other person a chance to express their side, you need to genuinely listen, so that you know where the other person is coming from and you can give valuable feedback.

Reach a Negotiation or Agreement

Ideally, after having a difficult conversation, two people can make concessions to satisfy each other on the issue or agree on a satisfactory change that will occur as a result of the conversation. When conflict ends in harmony, a difficult discussion turns into a resolution.

Managing Anger and Stress Quickly & Effectively

It's amazing how quickly background stress can become a normal part of everyday life. You really need to be doing activities to manage your stress on a daily basis. Meditation, yoga and physical exercise are great but what can you do when you are in the work environment 8 to 12 hours a day? The good news is there are certain stress relief techniques you can use throughout the day to help you manage your stress levels while having to deal with difficult people at work.

Breathing

Your breathing is closely related to how stressed you are. You can become aware of how you are breathing at any moment whether standing or sitting in a chair. To become more relaxed breath more slowly and deeply down into your stomach. Before breathing out pause for 2 seconds. Practice doing this regularly throughout the day for a couple of minutes each time and you will soon develop better breathing habits that lead to reduced stress.

Heart Wisdom

When we are stressed it's often because we have lots of thoughts racing through our mind. Our attention and energy is focussed on those thoughts. By changing our focus of attention we can move our energies into a more harmonious place. With scientific research being done by groups such as, The Institute of Heartmath, it's becoming clear that the human heart has it's own intelligence. You can tune into your 'heart wisdom' by simply focussing your attention on your heart centre for a few moments. If appropriate place your hands on your heart and then imagine breathing into this heart centre.

You will begin to feel more relaxed, balanced and in harmony within a few minutes.

Stress Fader

The more stressed you are, the more the 'fight or flight' response kicks in. This means that blood leaves your brain and goes into your muscles instead. What follows is a simple and very effective technique that enables you to bring the blood back into your brain so you can think straight again.

There are locations on your head known as Neurovascular Points. The ones we are going to use to help reduce the stress response are located an inch above the eyebrows; the bumps on the forehead. By placing the thumbs on the temples at the side of the eyes and then placing our finger tips on our forehead we keep the blood from leaving our forebrain. Even when you've 'lost it' holding these points brings blood back to the forebrain, which means you will be able to think straight again!

1. Lightly place your finger tips on your "O' My God!" Points (the neurovasculars), one inch above the eyebrows. You can also put your elbows on a table and 'hold your head in your hands.'

2. Place your thumbs on your temples next to your eyes.

3. Breath and notice the blood (pulsing) returning to your forebrain, enabling you to think more calmly and clearly. This can usually be done in less than five minutes.

Top Tip 1: You can hold just one neurovascular point with one hand and elbow on desk while the other hand holds a phone.

Top Tip 2: You can of course hold other peoples neurovasculars to help them de-stress.

Useful Principles For Effective Communication

Changing Our Own Perception & Behaviour Works Best

We can't change others but we can change our perception and our own behaviours which transforms the relationship dynamics.

All Behaviour Has A Positive Intention

This is a very useful point of view. You act as-if at some level all behaviour is (or at one time was) *"positively intended."* It helps you keep a more positive mind set when dealing with awkward people. Ask yourself, *"What could be the positive intentions (protection, attention, establishing boundaries, etc.) behind the behaviours of the other person and/or your reactions?"*

Separate The Person From The Behaviour

The positive worth of the individual is held constant, while the value and appropriateness of internal and/or external behaviour is questioned.

The Meaning Of The Communication Is The Response You Get

With this principle you take responsibility for communicating the outcome you want effectively to the other person. If you do not get the response you want keep changing your own behaviour/communication until you get the response you want.

Remember To Have A Sense Of Humour

Having a sense of humour is one of the best ways to safeguard yourself from the effects of stress. Don't take yourself and situations too seriously. Keep light hearted.

There Is No Failure Only Feedback

All results and behaviours are achievements, whether they are desired outcomes for a given task/context, or not. In other words you can always learn something from *mistakes*. Ask yourself questions such as, *"What can I learn from this?"*

The Perceptual Positions

What you are about to discover is the same communication secrets as used by Gandhi in his conflict resolutions, what exceptional therapists and coaches do naturally to gain deep empathy, insight and understanding and what the Buddha taught extensively for developing deep love and compassion.

Wouldn't you agree that in any interaction between two people there are two points of view, right? Well, yes, that's true and there is also a third point of view: Imagining the two of you over there interacting with each other.

These points of view can be called *Perceptual Positions*:

1st Position (Associated or Self Perspective)

Seeing the situation through your own eyes. You are primarily aware of your own thoughts and feelings.

2nd Position (Other Person Perspective)

Imagining what it is like to be the another person in the interaction. Imagine stepping into their body, seeing through their eyes, hearing through their ears, feeling their feelings and thinking their thoughts.

3rd Position (Disassociated Perspective, Neutral or Meta Position)

Take a detached viewpoint. Imagine you are looking at yourself and the other people in the situation, *over there*. Try different *camera angles* to gain new understandings. You could also take the perceptual position of God, Infinite Intelligence etc. for an interesting angle.

You actually shift between these points of view already at an unconscious level, but with conscious intent and practice you can learn how to solve relationship problems more quickly by gaining empathy, insight and rapport with the other person.

Have you ever had the experience of being in an argument with someone and found yourself dumbfounded by the other persons reaction? Go ahead and think about one of those situations now and run through the following *Jedi Mind Trick*. I think you might be surprised by what revelations come up...

How To Solve Relationship Problems With A Jedi Mind Trick

- Think of a time when you were in a situation with other people and you didn't and still don't understand their perspectives on whatever issues were discussed. (Examples: A meeting, an argument with someone etc.)

- Now run through this situation from 1st Position. This means looking at the situation through your own eyes and hearing through your own ears. Notice your feelings and any thoughts you have about it.

- Next step inside one of the other people present (2nd Position). Literally imagine being in their body looking out of their eyes. So of course you will be able to see yourself. Notice your feelings as you see and hear from this perspective. Become aware of any new learning's.

- Now move to 3rd position. Remember this is the 'neutral position.' It's kind of as if you are a camera observing everything. See/hear yourself and the others and notice any new learning's you can observe.

Top Tip: Try changing 'camera angle.' You can get almost limitless new perspectives. How about, "Getting above it all?", "A birds eye view?"

1. Useful Questions

When you are experiencing each perceptual position it can be a good idea to ask the following kinds of questions to gain insight into the relationship dynamics and communication:

- *"If I knew how to solve this communication problem,*

how would I?"

- *"If there were a solution, what could it be?"*

- *"What would you need to be able to achieve better rapport with this person?"*

- *"How would <Role Model> communicate with this person?"*

- *"Imagine a miracle had happened. What exactly would have happened? How would things be now?"*

If you've gone through the process you'll have new insights into yourself and you will have a better understanding of others too. Sometimes this technique can be quite a revelation, seeing yourself as others see you enables you to change your behaviour to something more appropriate if necessary.

The World Is Your Mirror

It's one of those curious things in life. Whenever we find ourselves having to interact with difficult people, when we dig a little deeper, we will often find out the problem is actually something within ourselves. The other person is acting like a mirror for something within our own self. This is very useful to know because it means we can take control for improving the relationship by changing our own attitudes and perceptions.

If you've tried out the *Perceptual Positions* exercise above you will have gained some insight into how you can change your perceptions for improved relationships. The following exercise, designed by Neuro-Linguistic Programming (NLP) Trainer Robert Dilts, is a special arrangement of the Perceptual Positions, with an added 4th position, that enables you to become aware of this *mirroring* experience that occurs in relationships. It's a really empowering exercise that enables you to access your inner resources leading to better relationships and communication. Give yourself 30 minutes when you first have a go with this exercise. Take it step by step and you will soon get the hang of it and be able to go through it quicker the next time...

2. The Meta Mirror

1. Think about the person you have difficulty communicating with. See them from 1st Position (Associated or Self Perspective). Name the trait that makes communication so difficult. e.g.) "over serious," "indifferent," "in denial," "arrogant," etc.

2. Now step back into the Meta Position: 3rd Position (Disassociated Perspective, Neutral or Meta Position). So looking at yourself and the other person in the in-

teraction, name your own behaviour in relation to the other person. e.g.) "judgemental," "irritated," "helpful," "inflexible," "scared," etc.

3. Become aware of how the way you are acting actually triggers or reinforces the behaviour of the other person. If you were not there could the other person continue his or her responses?

4. Think about other ways you could respond to that person. Maybe you have already tried to change your own reactions. What makes you continue to act in the way you do?

5. Now step to the side into the Meta 4th Position: In this position you can observe the relationship you have with yourself. Become aware of how you treat yourself in this interaction. e.g.) "judgemental," "tense," "impatient," "aggressive," etc. In what way is your response to yourself a mirror for what the other person is doing?

6. Staying in the Meta 4th Position, switch the positions associated with yourself: Put your 3rd Position reactions (the way you have been treating yourself) into the 1st Position (so that you have that level of response to the other person.) Put your former 1st Position responses into the 3rd Position location. Notice how this switch changes the dynamics of the relationships.

7. Now put yourself into the 'other person shoes.' Step into the 2nd Position (Other Person Perspective) and imagine looking at yourself from this persons perspective. How does your behaviour appear from this perspective? As this other person what do you want or need from that person in front of you?

8. Step back into revised 1st Position: Notice how your point of view, reactions and feelings have changed.

9. If needed you can continue to switch perceptual positions and add choices of responses until you feel the relationship is more balanced and functional.

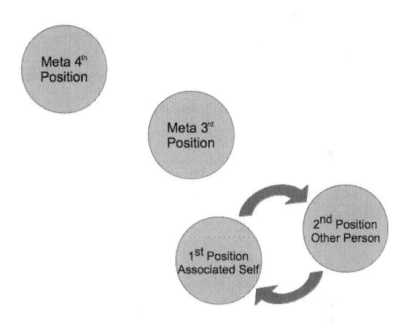

Getting Better At Dealing With Difficult People

Let's face it difficult people are always going to be around. They can make life very stressful but they do provide you with a great opportunity for personal growth. Spiritual masters from the ages have often considered awkward people as rare gems. There is a famous example of an Indian spiritual Master, Atisha, who had a cook as his travelling companion. Everyone knew Atisha's cook as a very obnoxious man to be avoided. However the spiritual master loved him because he helped him stay humble and down to earth with all his insults and coarseness.

If the cook accused Atisha of arrogance, heartlessness, or fakery then Atisha would have scrutinised himself, suspecting that the cook may be right. This is why the cook was such a precious gift to him. Atisha advised people not to think about their own good qualities but instead to think about the good qualities of others. He suggested not to think about the faults of others but instead consider our own faults and purge them as if they were bad blood.

By putting the information and methods shown in this book into practice you will increase your perception, change your own attitudes, reduce your stress, and add to your behavioural flexibility when dealing with difficult people. And last but not least; *Remember to have a sense of humour!*

1. Dealing With Difficult People Check List

- **Keep Calm**: Focus on your breathing and place your attention at your heart. You can place one of your hands on your heart if appropriate.

- **Listen Well**: Show respect for the other person by listening attentively and ask questions to help gather useful information to further your understanding of the person.

- **Practice Patience**: Your patience can always be improved and the fact is it's one of the best resources you have for dealing with difficult people.

- **Conversation Goals**: If you need to speak to a work colleague, who is difficult, prepare what you want to talk about before hand. Knowing the specifics will help you be more calm and coherent when conversing with them in person.

- **Manage Your Anger & Stress**: Practice the techniques for reducing stress and keeping calm and centred.

- **Step Into Their Shoes**: Practice the advice from, "The Perceptual Positions" chapter; Use the power of your imagination to step into their shoes and gain new insights into their feelings and perspectives.

- **The World Is Your Mirror**: Remember it's often useful, even empowering, to be aware of the way other people can be like mirrors for something within our own self.

Bonus Chapter: An Interview With A Conflict Resolution Expert

Ana Rhodes has been living and working in the Findhorn Foundation, a spiritual community in the north of Scotland, since 1994. During this time she has worked within a variety of areas in the organisation. She has been a member of the Central Management team over the last seven years, six of those spent being responsible for the area of Spiritual and Personal Development. This comprised of internal trainings, conflict facilitation, supervision and other internal structures that support the Findhorn Foundation to function gracefully and efficiently at an individual and collective level. In February 2009 she stepped into the role of Chair of Management/Focaliser of the Findhorn Foundation. When asked what her inspiration for taking on this position she said, *"What called me to take on this role was my deep love and desire to continue to serve and support the unfoldment of the Findhorn Foundation in the world as a Holistic Educational Centre, a Spiritual Community and a system dedicated to walking lightly on the planet."* Ana is one of the representatives of the Findhorn Foundation working in conjunction with the UN.

Ana is a conflict facilitation expert and has helped many individuals, couples, businesses and communities resolve serious conflict, misunderstanding and communication issues. She facilitates groups of up to 400 people in processes of socio-cultural and organisational change, using tools that support diversity and deep democracy. Ana is fluent in both Spanish and English and regularly runs trainings and offers consultancy in Spain, the UK, South America and the USA.

You can contact her here:

ana.rhodes@findhorn.org

The Interview

What was your motivation for learning conflict resolution skills?

Well my motivation, originally, was in my personal life; my background and my journey in life. Growing up in Spain, I experienced a huge level of conflict with myself and also my family and the Catholic culture. I experienced a sense of oppression as a young woman growing up in Spain; feeling like I had to follow lots of rules about how to behave, what I had to become in the future and the way I had to portray myself in the world. So from the age of about 6 years old, there were so many rules about how a woman had to be. So my journey with conflict started at an early age.

In my teens I got involved with drugs and rough, violent situations and ended up in the psychiatric system. I didn't really understand how to cope. I couldn't cope with life. At the age of 16/17 I had a very strong out of body experience with drugs. And at that time I came back from that experience and realised I needed to do something with my life that would be more useful. And so one of the key things coming out of that experience was that I wanted to be able to cope with the tensions of life; internally and externally in a more creative and loving manner - in a way that was more supportive for me and those around me.

How did you actually get started?

Well I arrived at the Findhorn Foundation; a centre for holistic eduction and a very diverse community and in some ways a spiritual centre. I got there when I was just 17 and for about a month I had no conflicts with anybody. But after this short phase all the conflicts that I'd carried with me from my personal history started to resurface. So after about 7 years living in the community and doing different jobs and running workshops, I was asked by Human Resources to become part of the team. And it made me realise I had no skills in working with people; I didn't know how to address conflict and conflict situations with people. So I realised that was the path I wanted to get trained on and that's how I initially became a student of Process Orientated Psychology (POP) in the States and in Ireland. I got started because I found myself in the work position having to hire and fire people, having to interview people and having to address human conflict without having a range of skills that were required.

What problems did you have to face in learning how to facilitate successful conflict resolution?

I think there are different levels of conflict I had to face. The first level were conflicts within myself; I had to deal with some basic, long term, internal conflicts about who I felt I was and who I wanted to become. In some ways some of the most important conflicts I had to address had to do with my own personality; the way I was behaving and my own belief systems. One of the key conflicts I had to address was to do with gender issues as a young woman. I had a lot of issues about oppression coming from Spain, so I really had to face that.

The other one that was really important was that before I could start working with others I had to face my own discrimination issues; coming from Spain, there are lots of racial and discrimination issues. At that point in my life I didn't think I was discriminatory but as I started working with different people I realised I had issues with people from other cultures due to my cultural programming from the media and society.

Another inner conflict had to do with my sense of values. Internally I was extremely judgmental about myself and who I should be; what a right or good person should be. And so I had to really address this because I realised I was really judgmental with others. So those were some of the first ones and then the other level that I had to face were interpersonal issues with other people. Because of course what happened is that one of the key areas I struggled with was with power and the way I used power, my own sense of power and the way others used power. So at the beginning I always used to feel disempowered when faced with conflicts. When I had conflicts with someone, I always felt the victim of them. I felt they were judgemental either because I was a woman, or because I was young, or that I wasn't good enough. So usually I wanted to retaliate and have revenge or basically I would feel like it was all my fault. It was either-or. I had to begin to face my own sense of power, discover my own natural abilities and how I could use my own power really well; not always feel less than others. And the moment I started to do that it was amazing how my relationships changed. The quality of my relationships became much more fluid, more equal, and I could give and receive feedback much better. Previously when anyone gave me feedback I would take it as criticism; it was a huge problem - I would either defend myself or over-apologise. So it was really important for me to step into my sense of power and value who I was so that I could stop feeling like a victim and be able to receive feedback in order to grow and develop, and be able to give feedback in a clear way. So all of this was actually at the heart of my development; the ability to give and receive feedback and not feel like a victim when criticised. These abilities gave me a sense I could grow as a person.

I come from a very Catholic background and in my family there are very strong women. It's a very Latino family. Women from a Catholic background have a complicated journey because they hold the families together but they are also very oppressed by the patriarchal heritage of the country. So growing up as a young woman I found it harder to receive difficult feedback from women than from men. When women gave me feedback I would immediately feel like I was not a good enough woman and it got very difficult for me to be able to receive feedback from women in positions of power. Even though I admired women in positions of power and thought it was amazing, I still found it very, very difficult. For me it was easier to relate to men and I found it easier the way men used their power because I found it more direct and to-the-point for me personally. The women in my family were very manipulative. So in terms of gender it was complicated for me coming from a Catholic background I really struggled with women's power and I found it extremely manipulative and oppressive. It took me a while, until I was older and more mature, before I could really develop healthy long term friendships with women. So it was always a little bit easier for me with men. It's quite common in Latino cultures that women are the worst enemies of women.

How did you overcome those problems?

I did a lot of inner work with the help of a coach and a supervisor that really supported me as a person. But I think the way I really overcame my problems was through learning to do women's team work. I ended up working in many groups with women so I had to learn to understand how to communicate with women in power. Also the other thing I did in my early 20's was to work a lot in South America helping women become empowered. With a colleague of mine we created the first women's commission group in South America. It was a committee of women that would work for the rights of women which had never happened before in that part of the world. For 5 years I went there for a month and a half per year and by living and working in that environment with women every day I learned to really understood the importance of collaborating with women and women's power.

Having said that I also think the good thing for me at that time in my life was that I also did a lot of mixed gender work in South America too and that brought in a lot of balance to the work. So it was an interesting journey for me. In terms of relating to men's power I had over many years worked with lots of men, in different positions of authority, and ran lots of different trainings with them collaboratively and it was always easier for me. I also think I'm the kind of woman that tends to be really direct and so it matches the so-called male culture a bit more even though that's really an illusion; not all men are like that of course.

One of the other things that was really important in my journey around conflict resolution was dealing with my own personal extreme states; dealing with my own personal health, especially around addictions and depression, such as the way I was using substances in order to feel more powerful. So as a professional I really had to dive deeply into understanding the deepest purpose of my life in terms of the way was I depressing myself and what it was at the deepest core of me that asked me to come through my depression and evolve. So really one of the most important things for me with dealing with conflict was to address my own shadow; depressions and addictions.

If you had to do it all over again, what would you do differently? Or more of or less of?

In terms of what I would do differently if I was to start from scratch I would have done more work with grassroots organisations from the beginning rather than later on like I did. So I would have been working more with "street conflict" and conflict that is happening around the corner of one's home. I think when we work with conflict in corporate organisations or NGO's or systems, the conflict has a contained parameter. But I think the basics of learning conflict work and the effects of violence, which are at the heart of conflict, you really learn in the streets. So I would have focussed more on this type of conflict at the beginning of my training. I run 3 year courses training people in conflict facilitation. And now when I train people, in the second year, one of their assignments is to go to the streets and do conflict work. For me this where a high percentage of congruent learning takes place because in that moment you really have to trust not just your skills but your presence. I think at the heart of conflict work the most important skill is not all your tools but the quality of your presence and the way you can stand still in the presence of a high level of heat and conflict. The street teaches you that; it teaches you to be very, very present when violence and a high level of conflict is there. And there is no controlled parameter or controlled laws about what can and cannot happen. So I would say for people that really want to work with conflict, they need to have the courage to visit diversity and area's of conflict such as the streets, the barrios, the ghettos, schools and the different religious churches. And they also need to understand how conflict works in the court of law. They need to visit these different environments and understand how conflict functions; to really feel the level of human tension that happens in these different everyday environments. So that's what I do now; I take my students to all these different environments and sit there and feel what happens there, which I didn't do enough of at the beginning and I'm doing it now.

The alchemy of conflict is the same across cultures but the style in which it appears is different with each particular culture. So you need the courage to visit and experience these different cultures. And I think this is really important and a lot of conflict resolution training doesn't understand that this cross-cultural awareness is at the heart of conflict facilitation. Like right now we have a lot of immigration laws, but the fact is we are living in an immigrant society. We live with people from different cultures that are neighbours with us. So I think experiencing diversity is really important. Many teachers of conflict resolution talk about diversity but they haven't actually experienced it; they haven't visited different places.

If you were to advise a close friend or family member how to follow in your footsteps for becoming an effective conflict facilitator, what would you tell them?

I would say start at home; start within yourself: What are the key conflicts you are travelling with in your life? And how is the quality of the relationships with those close to you? Evaluate those and start understanding your behaviour in terms of conflict at home. And have the courage to look at the changes that you need to address in order to intervene there.

So what would be the best way of going about that then?

I think you need support; the best way is to create some sort of support network or a team, or a school or learning community. You need a learning community that is willing to engage with you to understand conflict. You cannot understand conflict alone, you need support and a group of people that are willing to give you feedback about your behaviour and the way you encounter your context. Books and trainings are good but if you don't have a learning community around you the lessons aren't going to integrate properly. Being a good conflict facilitator has a lot to do with the integrity of your presence above all of the skills that you have. You may teach conflict facilitation but if in the process of teaching conflict you are constantly creating conflict then it's deeply incongruent. And when we say, "Yes," to being teachers of conflict facilitation we have to say, "Yes," above all to becoming a student of conflict. If you are not a good student of conflict, you cannot be a good teacher or facilitator. This is the thing that most conflict facilitators struggle with. At some point you start to think that you are above conflict and then what happens is that you start to misuse your rank and your power as a teacher. So you need a lot of genuine humility and as you teach conflict you need to continue to be part of a learning community that challenges you in keeping your learning up, otherwise you loose your humility and you become a very non-human teacher.

Conflict or points of tension in society or in relationships or at a personal level are moments of evolution for individuals, for groups and for society. Conflict is like love; love is a moment of evolution where your identity expands. And conflict also is a moment of evolution where your identity expands; not just your personal identity but a groups identity, a context identity, a cultures identity, a world identity and so forth.

In order to have the ability to stay present in moments of high intensity, which are moments of evolution, you need to be able to travel through different cultures and you need to have experience of being a participant in them. You cannot be a facilitator of those moments without understanding what it means to be a participant. Because behind the most difficult problems in this world whether they are political, economical or social - it's people. People can either make or break a whole culture or system. So as a person you have to have the humility to travel and participate in the culture and be touched and changed by the diversity of this world. That's why I think it's so important that part of becoming a conflict facilitator is to be a participant of places where diversity can really be experienced.

I've developed a whole paradigm between evolution, conflict and love; it's something I've been developing for a few years now and I've had different people give me feedback on it. It's about how evolution pushes through and how moments of evolution show themselves through tensions or through love. But it's the same experience; you experience heat and high intensity, and your identity in moments of love or conflict experiences a cracking; who you think you were can no longer sustain itself - you have to expand your concept of who you think you are. When you expand, your whole context expands because you no longer relate in the same way to individuals, relationships and the world.

So is this feeling of expansion at the core of what keeps you driven?

I think for me what is at the core of what keeps me engaged with the alchemy of conflict and of love is that in some ways it is very personal because I am interested in living well in my human relationships but I am also interested in dying well. So my desire is for co-creating community, freedom and viable relationships around me, my close circles and within this very diverse society that we live in. And I know that at the end of the day, weather I have a partner or not, I go to bed and when I close my eyes, it's me and my interaction with the world that goes to bed. So, for me, what keeps me engaged is my desire to understand the traction of love. Because for me love is an action; it's an action that is feely given - it has traction. And I think that at the heart of conflict there is the gold of synthesis and resolution which many people talk about as love. I am interested in viable cultures and viable relationships; relationships that respect diversity but can also co-exist together. Ultimately the day I die I want to be able to smile and look back on my life and say, "You know what I lived my life with a humble mind and an open heart."

If you want to become a conflict facilitator you must go back to the school of life and to the school of human relationships and cross-cultural relationships. You have to! You have to start from the science of human relationships; you have to understand key things such as how as a person you use your power and privilege; do you use them for your own benefit or the benefit of the many? You really need to go back to those basics in the school of human relationships.

What are your views on the so-called gender battle?

I think it's complicated because I think in terms of history there has been a massive disproportionate, out of balance, inequality with regards to gender power and gender privilege in terms of their place and status in society. So that is an historical journey that we carry for many generations in many cultures. Having said that it's changing; it's changing in many countries around the world. But I think right now gender is confused about gender power and gender privilege because we have changed the laws in terms of consensus reality, saying gender has the same privilege; men and women have the same privilege in terms of work and in terms of human rights. So we've changed the external laws but the psychological dilemma inside the power of gender is still in transition. In some ways I think women are learning about what it means to have power and what it means to have privilege in society. But sometimes I think they actually reduce it because they haven't yet learned how to use it properly. And men are coming to realise that they have over-used their power for generations and they are now confused about how to use it. In terms of family systems, many women now want to work; they don't just want to be mothers. So many things are changing now; we're in transition. We're having to re-adjust. Men and women are beyond the most polarised war; we're beyond shooting each other but we are still not sure what to do with our power, so we still create casualties. We're having to re-learn how to share power because we suddenly find ourselves with equal privileges but psychologically we are still having to battle. Men have been highly oppressed for over-using it and women have been highly oppressed for under-using it. And the thing is it's no longer really just about gender issues. Now it's more complicated because it's also about sexual orientation and identity issues. And we now have families that are no longer just based on a heterosexual partnership. So there are different ways of being in relationship and the same at work. There is much more for us to learn about power and privilege in terms of our gender and sexual orientation and how we use it well.

What do you imagine the possibilities of conflict resolution facilitation could be in the near future?

Well, I'm currently creating a centre in Spain dedicated to the transformation of human conflict. I think we are in interesting times in the world; there is a high level of conflict right now. We have many laws but conflict is escalating; there are more wars, we have a lot of conflict with the environment, we have financial conflict, we have conflict of leadership in many countries and we have a lot of social/cultural tensions due to immigration. So I actually think that conflict resolution needs to be one of the key educational classes that are given in school; from primary school onwards. We have to teach the younger generations the skills needed to resolve individual, interpersonal and social/cultural conflicts in our everyday lives so that we can prevent national conflicts and international long term destruction. This is no longer just necessary, it's urgent! I think conflict resolution has to be now a part of the education system. And not just conflict resolution but also the relationship between conflict and love; being able to build sustainable, viable communities. So if I had a high dream about conflict resolution and the relationship between conflict and love, it would be to bring this into the educational system from an early age because many of us are learning these skill much later on in life. So we could prevent a lot of conflicted interpersonal dynamics from an early stage. I think conflict resolution and building viable relationships is now an international political issue; it's not just a psychological issue of cultures. I think learning to welcome conflict and navigate it well has to be part of the political agendas of many nations, including the UN, as one of the requirements for leaders and politicians of all nations to engage with.

Also for a long time I wanted the world to change but I didn't want to endure the trouble of helping make that happen. It was so much easier for me to dream of better leaders who give charismatic speeches about community or civil rights, who promise improvement in the economy and the betterment of human kind. I use to think that society would, of its own accord, outgrow power and class structures. And so I sat and waited in the false hope that someone else will create a better world. But I have learnt that group transformation begins with me. When I realised that I as and individual could not separate my self from the communities around me, could not think any longer about me and them, it was the most inspiring and scariest of discoveries in my life.

To realise that I am because of you and that the world is because of me was and continues to be a deeply humbling experience. This means that is up to me to transform and change. It means that I do not have to become a Politician or a world leader to change the world. But it's also scary because it means that group transformation can begin today and not tomorrow or in the future when I know more about law or when I have more money or when I have a better education. *The thing is can I, can we, love and welcome all aspects of our selves?* My personal answer is that I do not. I can so much easily appreciate and feel good about the parts of me that are kind, respectful of others, caring, smart, educated, socially successful, funny, and so on. But it is very difficult to equally have compassion or dare I say love those parts of me that are racist, sexist, those parts of me that want to shut others down or that have hurt and verbally abused others, and to not judge myself when I feel depressed or vulnerable. So when I feel a victim of my relationships and life circumstances can I love and understand that underneath all this there is a story, a message that I need to hear so that I may grow in understanding, so that I may be able to sit in the fire of group diversity and not want to destroy the other, but be able to listen and become a part of the change I want to see in the world. I confess that I am scared to open the door when trouble knocks; I only want to let harmony in. But if I remember, if we all remember that when trouble knocks new relationships could begin. When trouble knocks, the possibility of a new kind of community is at the door. This new community is not only based on understanding one another, but on the common decision to enter in to the unknown, into the fire that transforms individuals, groups and social systems.

I would like to share a quote from Gandhi, he said, *"It is not about wining battles but about wining hearts and minds."* This, I believe, is the essence of the type of leadership that inspires individuals and ultimately societies to work for the good of the whole. There is only one planet Earth and the time has come to understand that we all have equal responsibility in the caring of it as well as for each other.

There is a great need in the world to rise to the challenge and start practicing a type of leadership that enables, supports and inspires. A type of leadership that at its core promotes listening and empathy. A type of leadership that it is not based on fundamentalism of any kind, for otherwise it will lead as to an old paradigm of dictatorship were someone always wins and someone loses, where the strong marginalise the weak, where minorities are ignored, were the earth's ecosystem is trashed and forests will continue to be burnt in the name of economical profits, where the big companies will take over the small ones, where the wisdom of our elders will be forgotten. If we don't wake up and contribute, if we don't dare to challenge our selves to welcome the reality of a diverse world that encompasses many different traditions, religions, cultures and world views, and continue to sit comfortably in our own homes waiting for someone else to do it, nothing will change.

Further Reading

- The 4-Hour Work Week: Escape the 9-5, Live Anywhere and Join the New Rich

- The Art of War

- EFT Tapping: How To Relieve Stress And Re-Energise Rapidly Using The Emotional Freedom Technique

Recommended Reading

If you found this quick start guide to dealing with difficult people beneficial, you will probably enjoy my 142 paged best seller, available on Amazon Kindle and in Paperback:

The NLP ToolBox: Your Guide Book to Neuro Linguistic Programming NLP Techniques

Made in the USA
San Bernardino, CA
23 March 2016